Introducing Continents

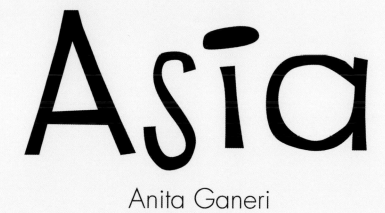

Asia

Anita Ganeri

Heinemann
LIBRARY

Chicago, Illinois

To contact Capstone Global Library please phone 800-747-4992, or visit our web site, www.capstonepub.com

Edited by Dan Nunn, Rebecca Rissman, Sian Smith, and Helen Cox Cannons
Designed by Philippa Jenkins
Original illustrations © Capstone Global Library Ltd 2014
Picture research by Liz Alexander and Tristan Leverett
Production by Vicki Fitzgerald
Originated by Capstone Global Library Ltd

Library of Congress Cataloging-in-Publication Data

Ganeri, Anita, 1961- author.
  Introducing Asia / Anita Ganeri.
    pages cm.—(Introducing continents)
  Includes bibliographical references and index.
    ISBN 978-1-4329-8039-9 (hb)—ISBN 978-1-4329-8047-4 (pb) 1. Asia—Juvenile literature. I. Title.

  DS5.G36 2013
  950—dc23   2012049491

Acknowledgments

The author and publisher are grateful to the following for permission to reproduce copyright material: Alamy p. 16 (© Shivang Mehta); Getty Images pp. 13 (Noel Celis/AFP), 17 (Mint Images/ Frans Lanting), 18 (Marketa Jirouskova/Oxford Scientific); Shutterstock pp. 6 (© Alexandra Lande), 7 (© Anastasios71), 8 (© my-summit), 9 (© David Steele), 10 (© stephen Rudolph), 11 (© ekipaj), 12 (© alersandr hunta), 14 (© Sergey Uryadnikov), 15 (© silver-john), 19 (© LIN, CHUN-TSO), 20 (© Dmitry Berkut), 21 (© shupian), 22 (© Hinochika), 23 (© Dana Ward), 25 (© Svilen G), 26 (© Stasis Photo), 27 (© Thomas La Mela).

Cover photographs of mountains in China, a Chinese New Year lion dance, and a shaded relief map all reproduced with permission of Shutterstock (© Vixit, © windmoon, © AridOcean).

Every effort has been made to contact copyright holders of any material reproduced in this book. Any omissions will be rectified in subsequent printings if notice is given to the publisher.

Disclaimer

Contents

About Asia. 4

Famous Places 6

Geography. 8

Weather. 12

Animals. 14

Plants 16

Natural Resources. 18

People 20

Culture and Sports. 22

Countries. .24

Countryside and Cities 26

Fun Facts 28

Quiz. 29

Glossary 30

Find Out More. 31

Index. 32

Some words are shown in bold, **like this**. You can find out what they mean by looking in the glossary.

About Asia

A **continent** is a huge area of land. There are seven continents on Earth. This book is about the continent of Asia. Asia is the biggest continent.

Asia stretches from the Mediterranean Sea
in the west to the Pacific Ocean in the east.
To the north is the Arctic Ocean. In the west,
Asia is linked to the continent of Europe.

Asia Fact File	
Area	about 16,919,000 square miles (43,820,000 square kilometers)
Population	more than 4 billion
Number of countries	50
Highest mountain	Mount Everest at 29,035 feet (8,850 meters)
Longest river	Yangtze at 3,915 miles (6,300 kilometers)

Famous Places

Asia has many famous places. Some are very old. The Taj Mahal in India was built more than 400 years ago. The **emperor** of India built it as a **tomb** for his wife.

The beautiful Taj Mahal is built from white marble.

Inside the Burj Khalifa are apartments and offices.

Some famous places are very modern. The Burj Khalifa in Dubai, in the United Arab Emirates, opened in 2010. It is almost 2,720 feet (830 meters) high—the tallest building in the world.

Geography

Asia has many different **landforms**. The Himalayas are found to the north of India and Nepal. They are the highest mountains on Earth. Mount Everest is the world's highest mountain. It stands 29,035 feet (8,850 meters) tall.

Many climbers visit the Himalayas every year.

Ural Mountains

Pamirs

Karakoram Range

Kunlun Mountains

Mount Everest

Himalayas

| 0 | 1275 miles |
| 0 | 2050 km |

Betpak-Dala
Desert
Gobi Desert
Syrian
Desert
Taklimakan
Thar
Desert
Desert
Rub al Khali

0   1275 miles
0   2050 km

One-humped camels
live in the sandy
Rub al Khali Desert.

There are enormous deserts in Asia.
The rocky Gobi Desert lies in China and
Mongolia. It is very hot in summer and
very cold in winter. The sandy Rub al Khali
Desert is in the Arabian Peninsula.

9

The Yangtze River in China is the longest river in Asia. It flows for 3,915 miles (6,300 kilometers) from the mountains in western China to the East China Sea. Millions of people live along the riverbanks.

The Yangtze River is very important for water, food, and transportation.

More than 130 rivers flow into the Caspian Sea, including the Volga River.

Asia also has many large lakes. The Caspian Sea, between Asia and Europe, is the biggest lake on Earth. It covers 143,000 square miles (371,000 square kilometers). It is called a sea because its water is salty.

Weather

Asia is so big that it has a wide range of weather. There are rain forests in Southeast Asia. They lie around the **equator**, where it is always hot and wet. In the far north of Russia, it is freezing cold year-round.

It is so cold in Siberia, Russia, that the ground is always frozen.

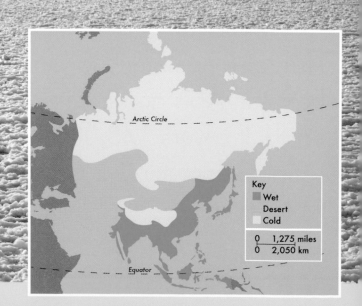

Arctic Circle

Key
Wet
Desert
Cold

0   1,275 miles
0   2,050 km

Equator

Typhoons cause terrible damage in the Philippines.

Each year, **monsoon** winds bring heavy rains to countries such as India. Some parts of Asia are hit by fierce storms, called **typhoons**. These can cause flooding that can wash away people's homes and crops.

Animals

Many amazing animals live in Asia. Orangutans live in the rain forests on the islands of Borneo and Sumatra. Komodo dragons live in Indonesia. They are the world's biggest lizards and can grow up to 10 feet (3 meters) long.

Komodo dragons only live on a few islands in Indonesia.

Giant pandas are easy to spot with their striking black-and-white coats.

Giant pandas live in south central China. They mostly eat **bamboo**. Giant pandas are very rare. Today, there are only about 1,500 left in the wild because their forest homes are being cut down.

Plants

Mangrove **swamps** grow along the coasts of India and Bangladesh, where rivers flow into the ocean. The trees have long roots to help them keep a firm hold in the mud.

Large mangrove swamps grow around the Bay of Bengal.

The giant rafflesia has the biggest flower in the world.

A huge forest of pine, fir, and larch trees stretches across the north of Asia. Warm, wet rain forests grow in Southeast Asia. The rafflesia is a rain forest plant. Its giant flower smells like rotting meat.

Natural Resources

Asia has many **natural resources**. Much of the world's oil comes from the Middle East. The oil comes from under the desert. The countries in the Middle East sell their oil around the world. Selling oil has made them very rich.

These oil wells are in the desert in the Middle Eastern country of Qatar.

There are many farms, both large and small, across Asia. Rice is grown in flooded fields called **paddy fields**. Farmers also grow tea, rubber, wheat, cotton, and sugarcane.

People

More than 4 billion people live in Asia. This is about three out of every five people on Earth. China and India are the most crowded countries. Very few people live in Mongolia.

People crowd along the banks of the Ganges River in India.

This is Chinese writing. The letters and sounds are called characters.

The people of Asia speak thousands of different languages. Many people speak more than one language. More than 1 billion people speak Mandarin Chinese. Some local languages only have a few speakers.

Culture and Sports

Many colorful festivals take place across Asia. Each spring, Japanese people celebrate when the cherry trees blossom. They visit parks to see the cherry trees, light lanterns, and have picnics under the trees.

These people in Japan are enjoying the beautiful cherry blossoms.

Many people play cricket in India and Pakistan.

Many sports are played in Asia. Cricket is very popular in India, Pakistan, Bangladesh, and Sri Lanka. **Martial arts**, such as judo and kung fu, are common in Japan, China, and North and South Korea.

Countries

There are 50 countries in Asia. The smallest country is the Maldives. It is a group of tiny islands in the Indian Ocean. Indonesia is made up of more than 18,000 islands. It is the world's largest group of islands.

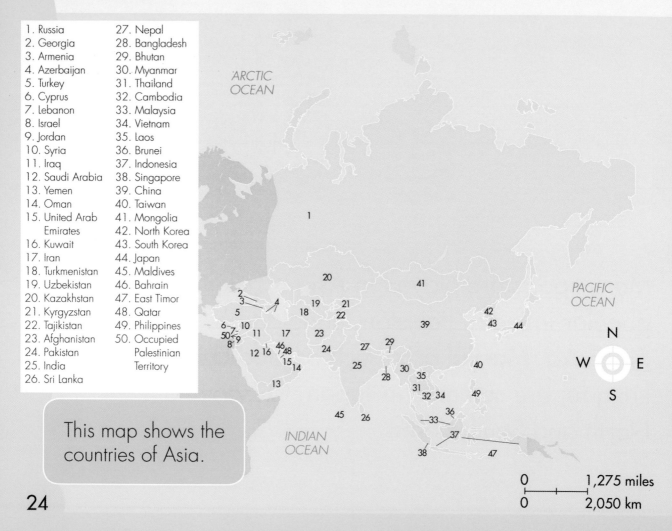

1. Russia
2. Georgia
3. Armenia
4. Azerbaijan
5. Turkey
6. Cyprus
7. Lebanon
8. Israel
9. Jordan
10. Syria
11. Iraq
12. Saudi Arabia
13. Yemen
14. Oman
15. United Arab Emirates
16. Kuwait
17. Iran
18. Turkmenistan
19. Uzbekistan
20. Kazakhstan
21. Kyrgyzstan
22. Tajikistan
23. Afghanistan
24. Pakistan
25. India
26. Sri Lanka
27. Nepal
28. Bangladesh
29. Bhutan
30. Myanmar
31. Thailand
32. Cambodia
33. Malaysia
34. Vietnam
35. Laos
36. Brunei
37. Indonesia
38. Singapore
39. China
40. Taiwan
41. Mongolia
42. North Korea
43. South Korea
44. Japan
45. Maldives
46. Bahrain
47. East Timor
48. Qatar
49. Philippines
50. Occupied Palestinian Territory

This map shows the countries of Asia.

0   1,275 miles

0   2,050 km

This photograph shows government buildings in Beijing, the capital of China.

China is the biggest country that is just in Asia. Russia is bigger but only part of Russia is in Asia. The other part is in the **continent** of Europe. Turkey is also split between Asia and Europe.

Countryside and Cities

In the countryside in Asia, many people still live in small villages. Some villages do not have running water or electricity. Each year, many people move from the countryside to the cities to look for work.

This small village is in Thailand. Many people who live there get food and money from fishing.

This crowded street is in Tokyo, the capital of Japan.

Asia has some very big, crowded cities. Among the biggest are Shanghai in China, Mumbai in India, and Tokyo in Japan.

Fun Facts

- Asia takes up almost one-third of all the land on Earth.

- Lake Baikal in Russia is the deepest lake on Earth. It plunges to more than 5,249 feet (1,600 meters).

- China and Russia have more neighbors than any other countries. China and Russia both have borders with 14 countries.

- The 10 highest mountains in the world are all found in Asia.

Quiz

1. Which building in Asia is the tallest in the world?

2. Which plant do giant pandas like to eat?

3. Which is the smallest country in Asia?

4. Which mountain in Asia is the highest in the world?

4. Mount Everest

3. The Maldives

2. Bamboo

1. The Burj Khalifa in Dubai

Glossary

bamboo tall plant with thin, woody stems

continent one of seven huge areas of land on Earth

emperor person who rules an empire

equator imaginary line running around the middle of Earth

landforms features, such as mountains, on Earth's surface

martial arts sports such as judo and karate

monsoon wind that brings heavy rain

natural resources natural materials that we use, such as wood, coal, oil, and rock

paddy fields flooded fields where rice is grown

swamps places where the ground is muddy or flooded

tomb place where a dead body is buried

typhoons fierce storms that bring strong winds and heavy rain

Find Out More

Books

Ganeri, Anita. *Exploring Asia*. Chicago: Heinemann, 2007.

Royston, Angela and Michael Scott. *Asia's Most Amazing Plants*. Chicago: Raintree, 2009.

Schaefer, A.R. *Spotlight on Asia*. Mankato, Minn.: Capstone, 2011.

Web sites

FactHound offers a safe, fun way to find Internet sites related to this book. All of the sites on FactHound have been researched by our staff.

Here's all you do:
Visit www.facthound.com
Type in this code: 9781432980399

Index

animals 9, 14–15
Arabian Desert 9
area of Asia 5, 28

Baikal, Lake 28
Bangladesh 16, 23
Burj Khalifa 7

Caspian Sea 11
China 9, 10, 15, 20, 21, 23,
    25, 27, 28
cities 27
continents 4
countries 5, 24–25
countryside 26
culture 22

deserts 9
Dubai 7

Everest, Mount 5, 8

famous places 6–7
farming 19

geography 8–11
Gobi Desert 9

Himalayas 8

India 6, 13, 16, 20, 23, 27
Indonesia 14, 24
islands 14, 24

Japan 22, 23, 27

lakes 11, 28
languages 21

Maldives 24
Mediterranean Sea 5
Middle East 9, 18
Mongolia 9, 20
mountains 5, 8, 28

natural resources 18–19
North and South Korea 23

Pakistan 23
people 20–21
Philippines 13
plants 15, 16–17
population 5

Qatar 18

rain forests 12, 17
rivers 5, 10, 11, 20
Russia 12, 25, 28

sports 23
Sri Lanka 23

Taj Mahal 6
Turkey 25

weather 12–13

Yangtze River 5, 10